Midge

My Life Story

Midge

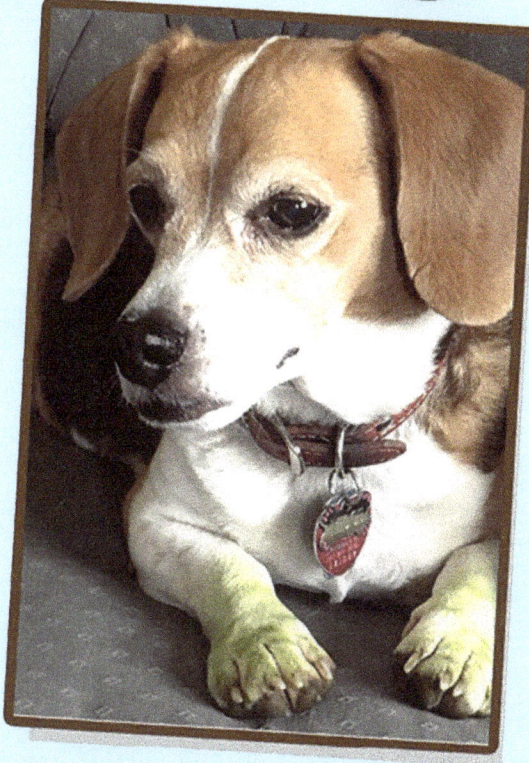

My Life Story

Beverly Koribanic

ARPress

ILLUMINATING IDEAS,
EMPOWERING VOICES

ARPress LLC
45 Dan Road Suite 5
Canton MA 02021
Hotline: 1(888) 821-0229
Fax: 1(508) 545-7580

Ordering Information:
Quantity sales. Special discounts are available on quantity purchases by corporations, associations, and others. For details, contact the publisher at the address above.

Printed in the United States of America.

ISBN-13:	Softcover	979-8-89330-482-4
	Hardcover	979-8-89330-484-8
	eBook	979-8-89330-483-1

Library of Congress Control Number: 2024901142

PREFACE

I'm Midge. This is my real-life story. Nope- I can't write but this was written by my very good friend. She was my third family. I hope you enjoy my story as I have enjoyed my life. I just wanted everyone to know to never give up and to be proud of who you are. We all have something to give to others and to learn from others. Yup- even dogs.

This book is dedicated to the old saying that beauty is only skin deep. Plus, the saying the strength lies within us. We all have a cross to bear and some of us have multiple crosses. Midge was a cute little dog that had many crosses to bear but you would never have known it if you met her. She touched so many lives in many positive ways. This book is dedicated to a very beautiful dog that overcame physical handicaps and the many changes/adversities in her life. She touched so many lives and was always greeted by the words "what a beautiful little dog". Her personality always shined through...Hopefully you too will be touched by her inner strengths and her inner beauty as you read each page...

Midge

My Life Story

Hi... I'm Midge... Yup, I'm a beagle.

I'm kinda small for a beagle and I'm not perfect but to be honest who is perfect?

I'm paralyzed on one side of my face, so my bottom jaw sticks out a little and my one eye looks a little lower than the other.

Plus, I am missing a bone in my hind leg when I was born so when I run —I kinda run on three legs and my tail is a bit crooked but I'm loved for who I am.

The Vet that I go to called me a misfit, he's silly. LOL

My first family named me Midge because they said I was a midget and I guess they were right.

I'm small for a beagle.

My first family liked to feed me table scraps and I liked to eat so I got a little chubby, but I was happy with them.

I lived with them for 10 years. But sadly, they passed away and I got another family, but they couldn't keep me because they had to move and the rental property they got wouldn't allow dogs.

So, they gave me to my third family.

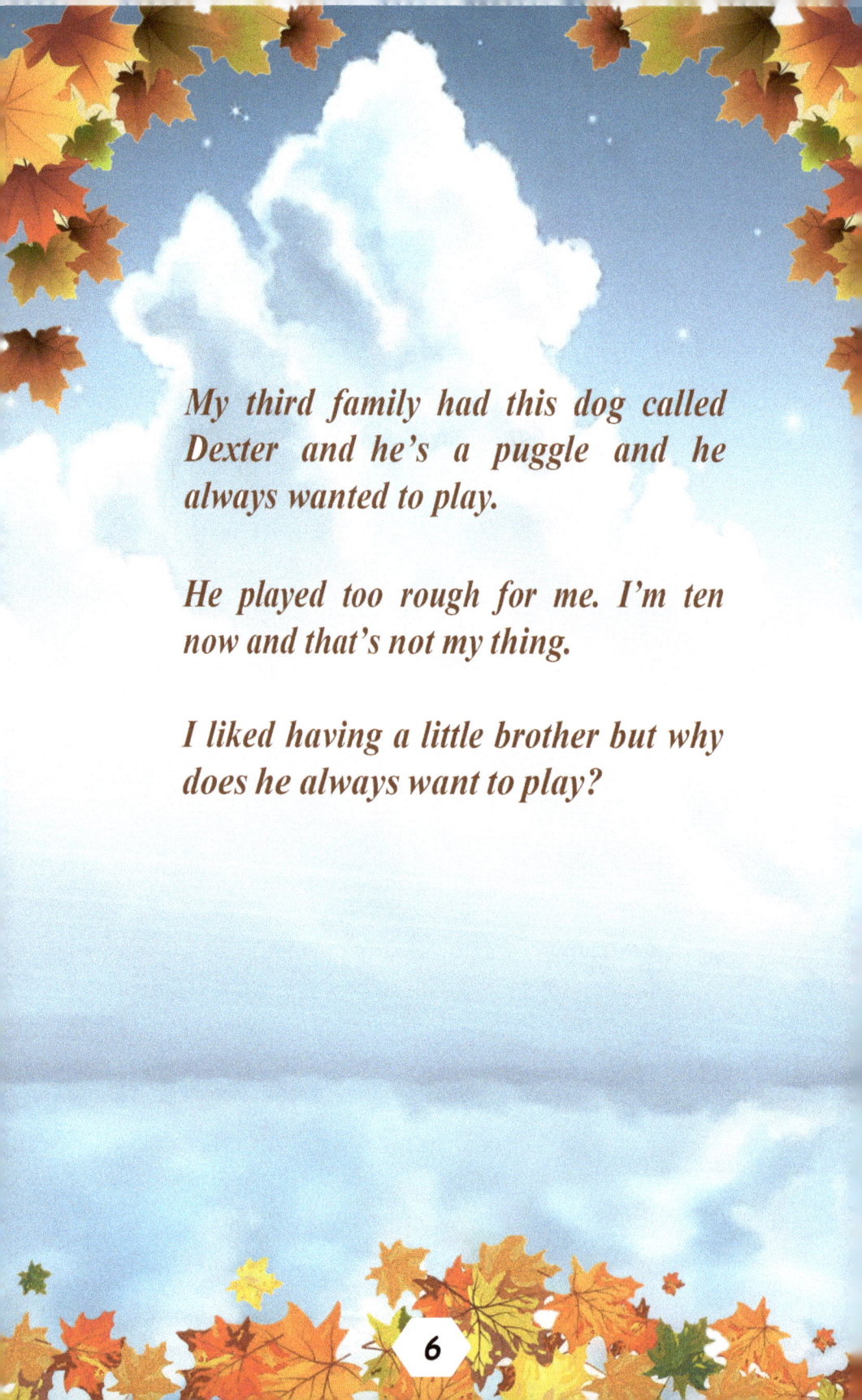

My third family had this dog called Dexter and he's a puggle and he always wanted to play.

He played too rough for me. I'm ten now and that's not my thing.

I liked having a little brother but why does he always want to play?

Yup....... That's Dexter!

I was kinda happy with my third family but not that much.

I tried to run away two times, but I got caught by my third family.

The first time I ran away. I kinda got out of my collar. She didn't have a fenced in yard so when she was out gardening, she chained me on a fifty foot leash. She kept her eye on me but when she wasn't looking, I slipped out of my collar and almost got away with it but I got to the parking pad and my legs were too small to jump down from the parking pad so she caught me.

She didn't learn too much so on another day she did the same thing but she made my collar a little tighter so I couldn't slip out. She was silly. I'm a beagle and I'm very smart. I slipped out of my collar again. I got down to the street this time and I didn't go on the parking pad. I learned from my first mistake. I heard her calling my name, but I kept running down the street. It was a busy street too. She called my name and was running after me down the street. I have tiny legs so she finally caught up to me and carried me back home. I guess I scared her because she was sad.

I guess I had some problems getting use to them.

The person I was with knew that I wasn't as happy as I could be and gave me to someone I really love.

He is really a very kind man.

He takes me on long walks, and he put me on a diet, so I slimmed down quite a bit. My first family fed me table scraps, so I was a little chubby---well I guess I was more than a little chubby. I had trouble losing weight. The long walks really helped me get more active too. I slimmed down quite a bit walking with my Dad.

I started to run and move more. Being active made me feel better too.

My Dad

We go on long drives to Ohio, as well. He lets me sit on his lap while he drives. I liked seeing the different sights and travelling with my big brother.

Oh, I forgot to tell you… I have a big brother now and his name is Dakota.

Dakota likes me being his little sister. He takes care of me too and watches over me. He's my travel buddy too. We both go to Ohio with my Dad.

I LOVE car rides.

I like smelling the fresh air and I like having my Big brother sit beside me.

He's kinda hard to see but he's beside me. See if you can spot him beside me.

Dad took me and Dakota to Canada and we went on walks there. There was a lake there too, but I was afraid to go in the lake for a swim. Me and Dakota just walked the dock.
That was fun.

Everyone says I'm cute which makes me very happy.

I like going on rides in the car. That's the best.

I like sitting in the front seat too and looking at my Dad.

But I still get tired sometimes…

I still visit with Dexter, too, as long as I can go back home to my Dad plus there's always food and treats when I visit with Dexter. I still like my treats.

Dexter still likes to run and play.

Sometimes I just like to hide my head when I want to go to sleep in the day so the sun is not in my eyes.

Sometimes I like being covered with blankets……

My Dad cares about me and covers me up.

Recently, I got sick. My Dad takes really good care of me but it's my kidneys.

My Dad and Dakota care a lot about me. Kinda hard to see Dakota (see if you can spot him) but he's there too and he cares too. My Dad looks sad but it's ok. I just can't tell him it will be ok.

I know I will have to leave him soon.

I'm fourteen now going on fifteen.

I'm trying my best to hang in there and he's trying really hard to keep me but... I know I will have to leave and I know it will be a better place.

I will be with my first family once again (I hope) and I know I will be happy there.

Life changes all the time. I will be sad to leave my Dad and my big brother but happy to be with my first family (I hope) and to have my next adventure...

Everyone loved me for who I am, and they never saw my faults. They all saw me and loved me as I am. I loved them all, as well. Yeah, I even loved Dexter.

www.ingramcontent.com/pod-product-compliance
Lightning Source LLC
Chambersburg PA
CBHW051253120626
46547CB00014B/1921